MORE THAN MAGIC

Discover Your Inner Power

Imagined by Bella Butler, Age 5

written by
Kate Butler

art by
Izabela Ciesinska

Kate Butler
BOOKS™

Confidence, Imagination and Dreams

Kate Butler BOOKS™

Created with love.

Copyright © 2014 Kate Butler Books
Library of Congress Control Number: 2015909280

www.katebutlerbooks.com

All photos by Chele Conway
www.cheleconwayphotography.smugmug.com

Design and text layout by Margaret Cogswell
www.spiderbuddydesigns.com

Edited by Mary Gorden

Printed in China

The book is dedicated to Teacher Mary.

. . . .

My grandmother, Mary Conway, taught me
to see the special gift inside each person.

My mother, Mary Anne Munning,
taught me how to honor my own inner power.

My grandmother-in-law, Mary Butler,
taught me the importance of family.

Once upon a time, there was a little girl named Maggie Mud. Maggie had magical rainbow powers that created all the colors in the world. Maggie's magical powers made the ocean turquoise, the fields amber, and the forest jade. The world was her canvas where she loved to create masterpieces!

But today did not feel like a magical day. Maggie was nervous that the children in her new school would not like her if they found out about her magical powers, so she kept them a secret.

Polly Puddles, Maggie's best friend, knew all about her magical powers. She was there the day Maggie discovered her magic! Even though Maggie and Polly were different in many ways, they always had so much fun playing fairy dress up, scooter racing, and jumping in mud puddles.

They especially loved swinging together. Polly loved to watch Maggie paint the sky!

Maggie was happy that Polly would be in her new school, but also worried because she knew Polly would make new friends very easily. Maggie was shy and not sure if the other children would like her.

On the playground Finley Fisher and his friends always seemed to be laughing and having fun, but Finley never invited Maggie to play along.

Walking home from school one day, Finley Fisher and his friends were whispering and laughing. Maggie felt ignored once again.

"My magic makes me different and I feel like I don't fit in," Maggie said to her Mom. "I just want to be the same as everyone else."

Maggie's Mom said, "Through Mommy's eyes you are beautiful inside and out. It's time to show the world what you are all about."

Maggie was very sad and did not want to return to school. She no longer wanted to use her magical powers to make the world a beautiful and colorful place.

The sadder Maggie became, the more the colors disappeared. One day, the world became black and white.

"What happened?" Finley asked. "Why have the colors gone away? And where is Maggie?"

Polly spoke up, "I think Maggie is upset because she feels different from everyone else. She doesn't feel like she fits in."

"Well, we miss her," said Finley. "It's not the same without her here."

Teacher Mary stepped in. "I believe Maggie was meant to add colors to the world, just like each one of you is meant to share YOUR special gift with the world," Teacher Mary explained. "When we don't share our special gift, we are left with a colorless world."

Polly smiled knowingly at Teacher Mary. Polly then said, "We need to show Maggie that we like her *because* she is different and that we are all different in our own way!"

"I have an idea," Finley said.

"Let's play the Magical Mirror Game." All the children had a piece of paper and imagined it was a Magical Mirror.

Each child looked into their Magical Mirror and said, "Magical Mirror please confide, what is my magic deep inside?"

To the children's amazement, the Magical Mirror reflected back each child's special gift! The children then drew a picture of their gift to share with Maggie.

When Maggie opened the door she was surprised. "You made these for me?" Maggie asked. "Why would you do that?"

"Because we missed our friend," said Finley with a smile.

Polly chimed in, "We wanted to show you it is okay to share your gift, because we all have a special magic inside!"

Maggie had been so worried that the other children would not like her, that she did not take the time to notice that everyone had their own type of magic inside. All this time the children just wanted to get to know the real Maggie!

Maggie remembered what her Mom said and knew what she had to do! She led all the children outside and began to color the sky!

She painted the trees. She put all the sparkle and light back where it belonged! When the color came back it was brighter than ever!

The children cheered! Maggie knew her friends were not just excited about the colorful magic. This was **more than magic**. They were happy to finally know the true Maggie.

Maggie's heart was filled with love.

The most important thing you can ever be in this world, is yourself. Everyone has magic deep inside. Each day is an opportunity to create new magic.

Be confident. Be bold. Be brave. Be YOU. And create lots of magic.

the best galoshes!

THE MAGICAL MIRROR GAME

my Lucky Ladybug!

Maggie Mud

1. What do you love doing the most? Painting purple elephants, riding my horse, and dreaming about a pet rainbow unicorn!

What's your answer?

peace!!

2. What comes naturally to you? Arts and crafts are my favorite thing to do! I love painting rainbows, drawing pictures with chalk, and making fairy houses!

What's your answer?

3. What have you always wanted to try? Oh, I would like to try a new art class! Maybe making pottery or watercolor painting?!

What's your answer?

4. How do you show others you care? By making cards with special drawings just for them!

What's your answer?

mommy! me!

5. What are some of your unique qualities? I'm pretty thoughtful, super creative, and I love helping my mom!

What's your answer?

Perhaps one day I will be an artist! or maybe a veterinarian. Maybe an artist who draws animals!

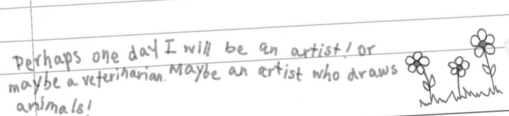

Magical Mirror please confide, what is my magic deep inside?

What do you think your answer will reveal about you?

CONTRIBUTORS

Author, Kate Butler / Creator, Bella Butler, Age 5

Hi friends! Welcome and thank you for reading. This book is especially close to my heart since I co-wrote it with my daughter, Bella. When she came to me at 4-years-old and told me she had an idea for a book, I listened, but I never expected to hear what transpired next. Bella went on to share a delightful story that soon became *More Than Magic*. I learned a powerful lesson in that moment: brilliance is ageless. You are never too young (or too old) to have a brilliant idea and make your dreams come true. This book is fulfilling both my dream and Bella's dream. From the bottom of our hearts, we thank you for being a part of it. In Bella's words, "I would just like each person who reads this book to feel magical in their own way."

I began writing children's books to create confidence, imagination, and dreams in children. In my first book, *More Than Mud*, Maggie Mud is born! We watch life unfold through the eyes of a mother and we learn how magical life can be with a positive perspective. *Mud* gives us permission to embrace the present moment, as muddy as it may be at times. Because even muddy moments can be blessings.

More Than Mud has remained on Amazon's best-seller list since it was first published in April of 2014. *Mud* also received the prestigious Mom's Choice Award® being honored for Excellence. Stay tuned for the third book in the "More Than" Series which will be released in 2016! Thanks to the readers and Maggie Mud fans, the "More Than" Series has turned into **more than books!** You can find *The Magical World of Maggie Mud* organic beauty products, magical art supplies, and inspirational creations at www.katebutlerbooks.com.

Illustrator, Izabela Ciesinska

From my earliest days in the crib, I longed for nothing more than to look at pictures and then draw them. As a child I absorbed every picture book I could - I read them all, drew them all, and I smelled all the pages. Soon enough I discovered the amazing world of animation, and eventually my ambitions evolved into film and illustration. Today I am fortunate enough to be working on multiple illustration and film projects.

Layout Designer, Margaret Cogswell

I discovered my love of layout design after landing my first "real" job at a publisher in 2012. Since then, I have designed over fifty children's books for some of the best clients in the business. My dream is to one day publish a collection of short fiction, which will meteorically rise to the top of best seller lists, and fund a round-the-world trip for myself and my husband.

BE MAGGIE'S PEN PAL

Free Stickers from Maggie
157 Bridgeton Pike
Suite 200, Unit #209
Mullica Hill, NJ 08062

Thanks for visiting my magical world. If you would like free Maggie Mud stickers, please send me a stamped self-addressed envelope and I will send you some!

Love,

MAGGIE